AS I LEARN TO WALK

5

AS I LEARN TO WALK

TO WALK

and other poems

JOE WALLER

Five Round Rocks Media

2018

Printed in the United States of America. For information, contact Five Round Rocks Media, LLC online at fiveroundroccksmedia.com.

Artwork design by Joe Fontenot, with design input from Joe Waller.

First Five Round Rocks Media paperback edition: August 2018
ISBN 978-1-71788-129-8 (paperback)

Published by Five Round Rocks Media, LLC.
www.FiveRoundRocksMedia.com

To Mom,
who let me take a creative writing class
instead of a math class

PREFACE

In college, I took a creative writing class. Instead of weekly readings, lectures, and discussions, we learned a bit about a specific type of writing, we wrote short pieces in response to prompts, then we read our work to the class and received feedback. I believe that's when my love of poetry really began. A free verse poem on Romans 5:8 (included in this book), a poem about the wonder of bacon, and a poem entitled "Manliness Explained" were my first three attempts to engage the art. Apart from a few off seasons, I haven't looked back since.

So why do I keep writing poetry? Why put words into patterns with rhymes and rules? Here are three reasons.

1. Writing poetry helps me process emotion.
I'm usually not the most emotional person in any circle of friends. At least, I'm not the most outwardly emotional person. I struggle to articulate what I feel, so I often keep silent. I struggle to work through my emotions, so I sometimes avoid engaging them. With

poetry, however, I can work through my feelings slowly, step by step. Writing helps me to sort out my cluttered mind and heart and see things a bit more clearly.

2. Writing poetry helps me clarify theology.

I cannot fully comprehend God. His ways are higher than my ways, his thoughts higher than my thoughts. The thought of his magnitude can overwhelm me. In poetry, I can consider him more methodically. As I look for the right word to fit the rhyme and rhythm of a poem, I must weigh every word's theological significance. Some words may fit the rhyme, but they don't fit God's character. Others may fit his character but not the rhythm. I've scrapped entire lines and sections because I felt that the words failed to accurately represent God. Writing helps me think about the Lord, and, in so doing, I pray I will grow to love him more.

3. Writing poetry helps me pray.

Often, my poems speak about God. They describe his character and his work in the world. At other times, my poems consider man. They examine life on this side of eternity. Sometimes, my poems are prayers. In these poems, I record my requests, my concerns, my realizations, my struggles, my joys, my hopes, my dreams. I lay out my words to the God who hears, organizing my thoughts before him and trusting him to listen.

Poems are like puzzles. There is joy in simply writing, satisfaction in feeling the page and the pen. I don't diminish that blessing.

But I pray my poems reflect more than simply a love of writing; I pray they reveal a vulnerable heart, a glorious God, and a child's prayers. I fail in these goals more than I succeed, but I keep writing, for I find great benefit in writing. And I hope the fleeting words I write prove helpful to you.

- POEMS -

A Prayer (As I Learn to Walk)

Deepen my convictions, Lord of heaven and of hell.

Quench my thirst with living water from the one, true
    well.

Let not my devotion be a mere religious act.

Let me learn to love you as a person, more than fact.

Tether me, O Trinity, to truth as unto air.

Marry truth to holiness and make my dwelling there.

Purge me of impurity, from all unrighteousness.

Privatize my worship. Let me work to serve, to bless.

Capture my imagination, my creator God.

Cultivate a true commitment kept by law and rod.

Let my life, in ev'ry aspect, be as unto thee

As I learn to walk with you for all eternity.

Grace-full Love

Redeemed-
Overwhelming the thought, that the
Master would love,
And not simply speak it,
Not merely masquerade it, but would
Show it, proving it in such a way that whether you are
5 or 50, you can still come to know this Truth
: One has saved, though we failed and fled His
    fellowship, He still came for
8's, 24's, 61's, 95's, and any age who answer Him with
    faith.

Meditation

Majesty, my plea for Thee:
Erase depravity in me.
Dissect my soul in stillness till this
Inconsistent life of illness
Tunes its life's song to Your key.
As I sit here silently
To meditate Your Word to me,
I seek for solace from distraction.
Open, heart, to holy action
Now. I pray for eyes to see.

The Christ

Behold the awesome power of the Christ.
Death cannot dictate where or when he goes.
No foreign threat, no wicked will, no heist,
Is able unto doom to him expose.
For from the Father from whose word all is,
He hath this charge, this holy, sov'reign right:
Authority to end his life is his,
And pow'r to take it back by his own might.
No creature claims dominion over Thee.
You are the Lord of all eternally.

Gospel

O Lord, I feel I stand as one alone,
Outnumbered far by fearsome fallacies.
Without, the monsters curse the God they've known;
Within, they call the monsters pharisees.
And I, although I know my eyes have seen,
Abandon light to look to darkest gain.
Forsaking wisdom, falling cured and clean
For fetching after fault and loss and stain.
I turn away from love to lovelesness
Inciting sin in spite of forgiveness.

For what I've done, I do not dare draw near.
For I, an heir, have spent his air to chase
Salvations proffered by this spinning sphere,
Solutions problematic to my race.
And now, though mind knows truth and heart knows life
And spirit sips the sanctifying stream,
Yet flesh forgets the food and fondles strife,
Yet yearns for filth far more than crossed beam.

Life seems to sit transfixed on sin and death,
Lifegiver laid aside for loss of breath.

So powerless, the weakness of the dust;
So powerful, the tendency to stray.
Surrendered now to sovereignty, I trust
Salvation's hope, though shrouded in decay.
The King approaches me, the rebel thief,
To lavish love and grace and mercy free.
He answers my despair with his belief.
He kills my death. He gives me eyes to see.
This central theme, this hope, I stand and sing:
This Jesus Christ, my Lord, my everything.

Life, true eternal, only found in one,
Lifts up my soul to seek the things on high.
The holy bread and wine of God the Son
Transforms my appetite for things that die.
Weak, I confess, my faith, my will, my love.
While I desire the depths, I stay ashore.
My lack finds his sufficiency above.
My sin, it reaches far; his grace is more.
I have naught but my sin to offer. He
Imputes his holy righteousness to me.

Now I, a vessel salvaged from the deep,
Not on my own behalf, do sail anew.
To save the souls still trapped and fast asleep

To lead them from the many to the few.
And this not by my strength nor will nor word.
All by him, for him, through him, to him—Lord
Of glory, glorified by trials endured—
Obtained by grace through faith all can afford.
My life is lived by light shone from the way.
My soul, he'll keep to stand upon the day.

For Christ has conquered Satan, sin, and self,
Forsaking for a time his form of light.
Though sold and slain for silver, bloody pelf,
The Son stole from the jaws of death the bite.
He, bruised and crushed, has crushed the serpent's head.
He, laid to rest, has satisfied the swords.
And he, by resurrection from the dead,
Appropriated us to be the Lord's.
Division, torn asunder in the veil.
Divinity in death did us avail.

Now, more than conquerors, we stand and fight.
No more are we the monsters of the dark.
For he has sparked our souls with his own light.
Filled by his Spirit. Carried in his ark.

Temptations have no power in his wake.
Transfixed are we on holy things above.
Desires of flesh forsaken for his sake.
Designer's glory - this the greater love.
O blessed Gospel! God has made me free!
O blessed Love of all eternity!

Thanatopsis

The time will come when mortal moments cease,
When breath will leave these lungs to come no more.
It matters not my state of war or peace:
Death still shall come to knock upon my door.
Then I shall greet him not as foe but friend,
For his is not the victory to gain.
Although, in time, my life doth seem to end,
Eternity my soul will then attain.
For I have died already, yet I walk,
Alive because the Word did more than talk.

Faith

Oh blessed joy of ignorance
As to what lies ahead
When fears assault my common sense
In search of steps to tread.
My future lies unknown to me
Beyond my line of sight,
And, as I look to what I see,
My heart is filled with fright.
This drives me to despair in hope
In what I can create
Until, as I in darkness grope,
I learn to sit and wait.
O blessed desperation which
Destroys the idol's hold
And shows me that I am not rich
In faith like saints of old.
O blessed pain that pushes back
Against my comfort's walls
And makes me see my state of lack
Instead of white washed halls.
Oh blessed trial that makes me know

I have no hope but one.
I can't complain if I would grow
In light of God's own Son.
My flesh is strong, my weakness vast,
My hope in self has died.
His love is proved from ages past.
In him, I shall abide.

Security

Though through the darkest valleys I
May pass in my pursuit of thee,
I will remember thou art nigh
And call to mind your love for me.

And though my path be wrought with pain
From broken hopes and shattered dreams,
I will find joy in you again
And rest in you by peaceful streams.

And though the sorrow may increase
Beyond all limits I perceived,
You are for me a constant peace,
The Lord in whom I have believed.

Though weakness and despair abound
As mortal flesh its limits reach,
In you, my strength afresh is found
As I your aid do now beseech.

A Joyful Cogitation

What beauty does exist for those
Whose lives are lost for better life,
For from the death of flesh arose
Freedom and vict'ry over strife!
In Christ, the perfect priest of hope
Indwelling all whom he has gleaned,
No devil now can interlope
Near to the souls the blood has cleaned.
A joy now reigns in time of loss,
And loss of all is highest gain.
Salvation—that the crux, the cross—
Succeeded in the Savior's pain.
Pure now, the slate of sinful man,
Purged by surrender to the King.
"Repentance! Glory! Heaven's plan!"
Redemption opens lips to sing.
Destruction now cannot destroy.
Despair no longer holds its pow'r.

Temptation fails to be a ploy
Though hell should loose itself this hour.
Christ's work has won a life of peace.
Creation's hope we recognize.
Old, earthly treasures we release.
Onward we march. On to the prize.

Wondrous Redemption, Mysterious Mercy

What kind of God would answer sin
With mercy, grace, and love?
Who pardons one so dark within
With blood from one above?
What Lord would take the rebel wretch
And make of him a son
While sending his own son to fetch
Through death the wicked one?
How can it be that I should see
Your love on full display
When, even as I follow thee,
I still do you betray?
I stand in guilt before your throne;
You throw my sin away.
You say I'll never be alone;
Your Spirit here will stay.
O Lord of all, I worship you
In spite of who I am
For who you are and what you do,
O sacrificial Lamb.

Let Me Be Found Faithful

Let me be found faithful
In the task at hand,
Working so to never earn
A word of reprimand.

Let me always listen
To the Master's voice,
Never speaking ill of him
But learning to rejoice.

Let me walk in wisdom
Each and every day,
Knowing that apart from Christ
There is no other way.

Let me know my limits,
My true state to see,
Resting in the love of God
In sweet humility.

Let me walk in freedom,
Nevermore to sin,
Following my Savior till
I die to live again.

Count it all Joy

The tragedies and maladies of life
All serve a saving purpose for the saint,
For struggles that surmount a life with strife
Become the hues with which our Lord doth paint.
O'er ev'ry evil, Elohim prevails,
Effulgent Savior, holy thaumaturge.
From death's embrace, the true Messiah hails
And makes what brought despair to heal and purge.
Now watch as broken daughters rise to dance;
Now see as sickly sons stand up to praise.
The vilest horrors help to fix our stance.
The worst oppression only lifts the haze.
No pow'r is held by any enemy.
All things do work as one for good to me.

Glorious Weakness

And so the Master bids me look within–
A blessed introspection of the soul–
To show me that the sinner saved from sin
Still lacks the strength and skill to take control.
Consistency of faith and focus lies
Within my hope but not within my hand,
For, though the goal is set before my eyes,
I have no pow'r to meet its full demand.
Yet I am found sustained by God above.
My only off'ring: insufficiency.
And as I face my lack, I find his love.
Oh paradox of this humility!
Herein I find the force to run the race:
His all sufficient, sacrificial grace.

A Fellowship of Love

Unbroken though the hammer falls
Upon this heart of stone
Within my flesh and bone.
And now I watch the walls
Undone before the holy war,
This siege upon my death,
Implanting righteous breath
And breaking down the door
Long under lock and barricade.
I ran from needed life,
Avoided peace for strife;
My heart by sin was stayed.
And yet the stone began to beat
By miracle of grace:
His glory filled the space
And left me no retreat.

And though transcending far above,
The Lord has made a way:
Communion here to stay,
A fellowship of love.

Questions

Is God still good when I have been so wrong?
Or, when I'm wronged, does love still win the day?
I read that he is with me all along,
But can it be when pain and sorrow stay?
Or might it be that his exalted might
Is meant not to pluck out but to uphold?
And could it be my eyes (so weak of sight)
Cannot perceive his plan of ages old?
Could he be working all things for my good
Although it seems that he is nowhere near?
Is this my furnace, this my cross of wood,
That shows me through my death that God is here?
How can I then bemoan the fiercest throes,
The holy forging, sanctifying blows?

Discontentment

"The grass is always greener..."
So they say.
So it seems.
"If I could only get there..."
Wand'ring mind.
Wishful dreams.
"My troubles would be over..."
Hopeful claim.
Happy lie.
"My life would be far better..."
Boastful joke.
Bitter sigh.
"If God would only bless me..."
Foolish talk.
Fallen heart.
"I'd give him all the glory..."
Downward gaze.
Devil's dart.

"So clearly can my eyes see..."

Captive soul.

Cursing breath.

"No chance of idolatry..."

Grasp for prize.

Grip your death.

The Voice of Temptation

Bask in your infatuation.
Nevermind your mutilation.
Spit on Christ's propitiation.
Carry on with sin.

Take the saving cord; unwind it.
Other souls will surely find it.
Jesus surely wouldn't mind it.
Let the devil win.

Seek ye first your own desiring.
Think not of the Lord's perspiring,
Nor of hell's eternal firing.
Run away again.

Surely God was only joking.
Gorge without a fear of choking.
At the beast we go a poking.
Let the games begin.

Victory

All you who fear the Lord of all
Have nothing in this world to dread.
Although, in time, your face may fall,
Eternity will crown your head.
Remember what our God has said,
That evil will not win the day,
For God in Christ for justice bled
And took the weight of law away.
Redeemed, we walk the narrow way
Through valleys cold and forests dark.
Onward we march into the fray
Approaching death, the final ark.
And as we on this road embark
And set our eyes upon the Son,
We pass the souls who bear the mark
Who from the light of love do run.
These journeys we have just begun,
Yet, shortly, they will be complete.
The wicked, then, will be undone;
The righteous, then, their Savior meet.
All kneel before the judgment seat.

All bow before the Lord's decree.
All evil he will there defeat.
His glory all mankind will see.
So do not fear the enemy,
Nor worry when he seems to win,
For God will have the victory
And he will make an end of sin.

The Almighty

You are the truth in a time of confusion.
You, the reality in the illusion.
Strength and supply for the weak and the weary.
Steadfast in wisdom with every query.
Faithful and flawless, you are the defender.
Fixed as the victor, you never surrender.
Perfect in holiness, pure in your vision.
Power and glory demanding submission.
Reigning in sov'reignty; rivaled by no one.
Revelation of the heaven you open.
Gracious and merciful, ever forgiving.
God: ever light, ever love, ever living.

Matthew 7:21-23

Follower:

Into a converse we now look

Between the Master and the crook.

Relationship the man mistook;

Now caught is he by fatal hook.

Man:

We kick and cry and curse and fight

Against the rain, the pain, the night,

As all offenders face our spite,

For we have surely earned the right.

How long, O Lord, have we obeyed?

Our flesh, though tempted, has been stayed.

To you for blessings we have prayed.

Are these, our lives, mere games you've played?

Wake up, O God, and serve our will.

We stand here waiting bored and still.

We've done enough to not be ill.

Come down; our lives with pleasure, fill.

Or we may cease to worship you,

No longer live as Christians do,

So think, dear Lord, and now come through.
We give you to the count of two.

God:
O child, you claim to know me well,
Yet cannot see how far you fell.
You still are under Satan's spell,
So listen to the truth I tell:

You kicked and cried and cursed and fought
Against my Son, your King, for naught.
He never sinned, yet blood you sought.
His rights laid down; your freedom bought.
How long, O man, have you betrayed,
While I my holy wrath have stayed?
Your sin upon my Son was laid.
Transgressions: just a game you've played.
Now tell me, just what is your will
That makes you apathetic still?
I gave myself, your life to fill,
And still you dare complain of ill?
What need of mine does worship meet?
Which quality is not replete?
You claim to walk with propped up feet.
You never knew the mercy seat.
No longer hold this foolish pride,
This heart of stone you keep inside.

To give you life, my Son has died.
Once saved, in him remain, abide.
Repent and turn away from sin.
Deny yourself, let life begin.
Embrace my love and enter in,
Or you will die to die again.

Follower:
Two voices speak across the span.
One hope to 'scape the timeless ban.
The mirror shows the person: man.
The Gospel shows the Father's plan.

Awestruck

How can eternity be fit into
A heart wrapped up in temporality?
Can lying lips do justice to the true?
The finite comprehend infinity?
We quake before the whispers of his ways.
Who then could stand before his thund'rous might?
This God who is, the all-consuming blaze–
He dwelleth unapproachable in light.
And yet, in Christ, the Maker made a way
For mortal man to know immortal love.
And beauty–more than words could ever say–
Became the revelation from above.
Communion takes the place of death in sin
As God makes blinded eyes to see again.

Paradox

Counted righteous, yet we sin.
Broken, but he lives within.
Dying daily while we live.
We are paupers, yet we give.
Owning, but cannot afford
Wealth belonging to the Lord.
Rich beyond all human dreams.
In the desert, finding streams.
Walking from the state of death.
Lungs of dust inflate with breath.
Weakness shows a deeper might.
Faith replaces eyes for sight.
Hope endures when hope has died.
Tortured souls in peace abide.
Counting joy the deepest strife.
Dying son; eternal life.

... To the Praise of his Glory

Let me walk...

Let me stay...

Let me talk...

Let me pray...

Let me know...

Let me cry...

Let me grow...

Let me try...

Let me yearn...

Let me reach...

Let me learn...

Let me teach...

Let me give...

Let me breathe...

Let me live...

Let me leave...

Return

Wake the slumb'ring soul within this man.
I have wandered far from my first love.
Living by my world-influenced plan,
I have lost my taste for things above–
Not that God's salvation was in vain,
Nor have I been stolen from his hand.
My old flesh, however, doth remain,
Warring 'gainst the grace in which I stand.
I, like Paul, do feel the fight inside,
Flesh and spirit trading blows within.
Though my Lord now calls me to abide,
I bypass escape to fall to sin.

No more.

Resuscitate me from this momentary lapse of
    consciousness.
I long to leave these lesser things and live in hope and
    holiness.

My eyes have seen the glory of the risen, reigning,
    coming king,
So let my feeble breath be brought before you as an
    offering.

Set my eyes on things above.
Bring me back to my first love.

Conform Me

Let me learn to love your voice.
Help me look to things above.
Save me from the selfish choice.
Show me how to walk in love.
Lead me in the way of truth.
Break me from the idol's hold.
Keep me from the lusts of youth.
Make me, for your kingdom, bold.
Help me keep my vision clear.
Make me humble, meek, and pure.
Help me know that you are near.
Let me, for your name, endure.
Make me always quick to give.
Let me ever testify.
Teach me how to truly live.
Teach me how to truly die.

Upon the Sea

My life is not what I had thought 'twould be
When I thought future thoughts in yesteryear.
I saw as if upon a serene sea
And set the sail with very little fear.
In hope, I left to follow heaven's way,
Believing that the path I saw was set;
But storms of life began to cloud the day
Until the plan I knew I did forget.
So have I learned to let the rudder keep
Within the hand of one who knows the course:
The savior and the shepherd of the sheep.
He is the destination and the source.
I need not fear though faced with darkest night.
By grace I sail through faith and not by sight.

Count It All Joy

Oh how quickly we abandon
Our morality and will
When, to our complete confusion,
Circumstances strike us ill.
Ill-advised is our rebellion,
Yet the rebel's part we play:
From disciple into hellion
When the storm invades the day.
Can we not remember glory,
That our Lord has won the fight?
Do we yet forget the story:
Light has broken through the night.
Suffering is light and fleeting
When compared to Christ above.
No bereavement, bane, or beating
Breaks the grip of God's great love.
Persecution serves to purge us.
Suffering now sanctifies.
We are bought by Christ's own purchase,
Seeing now with open eyes.

Therefore, we count joy our sorrow,
Singing praise in deepest pain.
Should we face our death tomorrow,
Even this is wond'rous gain.

Truth and Heresy

There never was a "then" when Christ was not,
Only begotten God of God on high.
The gospel story ever was the plot:
The spotless lamb for spotted sheep to die.
By nature, men do sin and stand in need
And lack the merit morally required.
And thus, the holy call, "Take up and read,"
Can offer life so lovingly acquired.
The Word was written that we might not sin,
That living branches might bear fruit for life.
Yet when we falter, there is hope again
As Christ called Peter thrice from Peter's strife.
We read and write for right theology,
That saints would not be swayed by heresy.

Grace

Grace beyond what sinful men deserve.
Grace that moves this salvaged soul to serve.
Grace that opens eyes to truly see.
Grace that works in love to pardon me.
Grace that guides my steps toward the goal.
Grace that takes the wreck and makes it whole.
Grace that reaches further than my sin.
Grace that opens fellowship again.
Grace that knows the longings of the heart.
Grace that causes hearts of stone to start.
Grace that this, my life, is not a loss.
Grace that gave his life upon a cross.

Christmas

The king was troubled in his soul
As news was told of kingly birth.
He spawned a plot to keep control,
Consumed with thoughts of his own worth.
But even in his selfish ploy,
He could not stifle heaven's plan.
Despite the sons he did destroy,
He did not stop good news to man.
For God so loved the world.
For God so loved the world.
From long ago the Lord has said
That he would send a saving son
To stand upon the serpent's head
And bring new life to ev'ry one
Who followed after Adam's way
In breaking heaven's holy law.
Messiah came to bring the day,
To rescue men from sin and flaw.
For God so loved the world.
For God so loved the world.
Though earth was lost in darkest night,

The souls of mankind dead and still,
The darkness saw a holy light
It did not, will not, cannot kill.
Now gone: defeat, despair, and death,
For hope and life and peace he brings.
He fills our lungs with living breath.
With triumph, ev'ry voice now sings:
For God so loved the world.
For God so loved the world.

New Year

The days increase that make up time behind,
And days unknown to us now lie before
Our feet, whose steps we never can rewind,
But must advance through this now open door.
The times around us change with each new day
Regardless of our feelings for the change.
Unsteady is the ground we wish would stay;
Our lives seem always set to rearrange.
But steady and unshakeable is truth,
And most dependable is God above.
For all the elderly and all the youth,
The constant in the universe is Love.
So hope as this new year begins to dawn,
And trust the Lord whose reign goes ever on.

Assurance

What God has spoken then
Seems lost before the now.
The call to enter in,
Eclipsed before the how.
The weight of life doth wear
Upon the focused brow,
But God knows ev'ry care.
He ever keeps his vow.

So trust we now our King
And hope in his command
And with the angels sing,
For he has made us stand.
We do not face his wrath,
Eternal reprimand,
For we now walk his path,
The purpose he hath planned.

Though circumstances prod,
Fulfillment we shall see,

In spite of shield or sword
Or strong desire to flee.
Thus says the Lord our God,
And thus it comes to be.
The promise of the Lord:
Reliability.

Logos

To think a parchment marked by nib and ink
Contain the cautions of a holy curse
And riches rivaled by no ruler's purse.
The scratches of the quill upon the page
Tell stories of the only perfect sage.
Come to the flowing fountain then and drink,
And find the firm foundation from the flood.
Be buried by the bounty of the blood.
The crossroad of your life is at the cross.
Be brought to life and lose the life of loss.
The message of the maker is the man.
Find pardon, peace, and purpose in his plan.

A Prayer to Hear

I serve a God who speaks-
Who speaks for me to hear.
And though his Word means life and love,
I rarely lend my ear.

    Yet still he calls me as his own.
    He grants me access 'fore his throne.
    Such love and grace to sinners shown!
    Oh help me, Lord, to listen.

The world with wailing reeks,
Wreaks havoc with its cries.
Though tinged with tones of great delight,
They only offer lies.

    For underneath the white-washed skin
    The dying soul cries out in sin,
    And wonders, could it live again?
    Oh help me, Lord, to listen.

I, therefore, need to pray-
To pray to hear his voice—

The whisper in the wilderness–
To make the holy choice.

> For Christ has died in my own place
> And given me a son's embrace.
> Oh let me look upon his face.
> And help me, Lord, to listen.

To Worship and to Fight

I feel temptation's throes around me now.
My heart is being beaten by the brute.
This flesh would see me finished with my vow.
Cry vengeance, God, and cut it at the root.
Too long have I now struggled just to breathe.
Too long have I imagined life is jest.
The holy Sword of God I must unsheathe,
And drive the blade into my very chest.
Cut out the heart of stone, O Lord of hosts,
And bring the dead to life by sacrifice,
For Christ has come to walk among the ghosts.
He paid with his own blood the ransom price.
O resurrected warrior of light,
Raise me now up to worship and to fight.

Sharpening

How can I comfort those who mourn
Unless I learn to mourn myself?
For fellowship with those forlorn,
I must be taken from the shelf.
For there I sat so safe and calm,
But there I also gathered dust.
If this, my life, would be a balm,
Then I must learn that God is just
Not just in times of peace and rest,
But in my sorrow, sickness, strife.
If I would follow heaven's best,
I will not have an easy life.
But through my broken heart, he speaks,
And through my suff'ring, Christ is seen.
If soon, with death, my body reeks,
My soul, by grace through faith, is clean.
So why would I avoid the pain
If, through the turmoil, faith is grown?
The struggle leads to priceless gain
As man's despair is overthrown.

All things do work together for
The good of those he called in love,
And though we walk the road of war,
God reigns in sov'reignty above.

O Heart Like That of Jonah

Is anger justified in you
Who sees your plans frustrated?
Who feels your life berated?
Whose choices are debated?
Do you do well to take the hue
Of anger in your manner?
Of squalor as your banner?
And rage against the planner?
Are there no better fights to fight
That you should mourn the passing
Of selfishly amassing
These treasures unsurpassing?
Are you so blinded by the night
That fleeting follies fill you?
That Jesus does not imbue?
That you forget your rescue?

Salvation

O God, I humbly must confess
My love for all unrighteousness.
My love for you, I know, is less
Than my desire for filthiness.
And I, by my own might, cannot
Erase the blemish, ban the blot
Of sin. This wound I cannot clot.
Apart from help, this life will rot.
So come before this heart of dross
That festers underneath the gloss
Makes of this man a total loss.
O God, how I deserve that cross.
I know there is no good in me.
Your son, I could not hope to be,
For by your word, I better see:
My only hope must come from thee.
And though I cannot earn your peace,
By grace you do from sin release
My soul, and cause my death to cease.
Your holy blood has washed my fleece.
Depravity cannot repel

The savior snatching souls from hell.
And though we wear this dying shell,
Our ears will hear the wedding bell.
So let me never now lose sight
Of your great glory, grace, and might,
And let your holy, saving light
Shine through and make me ever bright.

Who Is A God Like You?

Who is a God like you
That you should hear our cries,
And pardon our iniquity,
And never speak in lies?
Who is a God like you
That we are not too small
For you to stoop and seek and save
Our souls from our great fall?
Who is a God like you
That you should suffer loss,
And leave your throne to bear the curse
Of sin upon that cross?
Who is a God like you
Who overcomes our death,
And makes the broken heart to beat,
And gives us saving breath?

The Humble Ruler

The humble ruler born to die did come
Desiring not the trappings of a king.
Far greater than all earthly glory's sum,
He entered his own world through suffering.
Presuming not to take the place of prince,
He lived instead a life of sacrifice.
His poverty did make the wealthy wince,
Yet he was fit to pay the ransom price.
So well acquainted was he with our grief,
Afflicted by the wrath of God above.
The silent, slaughtered lamb has won relief,
And, by his wounds, he heals our hearts in love.
In service did the master live and die
And rise to rescue lost ones from the lie.

My Misunderstanding

"Be still," you say, "and know that I am God."
But know ye not, my Lord, that I must move?
I dare not halt or tarry as I trod,
That daily I might my devotion prove.
I have no time to sit and talk with thee
For there are souls who do not know your love.
You simply need to grant my ev'ry plea
That I might win more souls for heav'n above.
I, Lord, like Martha, see the work to do,
And I, to honor you, would give my all.
I would be known by men as ever true.
I need no other quest, no further call.
You justified me, Lord, by thy good will.
I need naught else, so you can now be still.

The Tragedy

A dozen knights in finest armor rode
To kill the dev'lish creature of the deep.
From citadels celestial, by the code,
They journeyed for the safety of the keep.
The party claimed allegiance to their king,
And gladly did they march for him to war,
Until they found the lands of which none sing,
For there they met the monster of the moor.
The beast fought not with sword nor spear but voice.
It promised untold riches for a knee.
And, one by one, the soldiers made the choice,
They each were felled without the faintest plea.
None were dissuaded by the death of friends;
Such is the tragic end of selfish ends.

Apathy I

We do not mind the poison as
We take another sip.
We do not mind the crushing as
We cast a biting quip.
We do not mind the gasses as
We take another breath.
We do not mind our dying as
We deal in deeds of death.
We do not mind the cutting as
We grasp another knife.
We do not mind the screaming as
We take another life.
We do not mind the sickness as
We eat the rotten meal.
We do not mind the hurting as
We pretend not to feel.
We do not mind the dulling as
We twist his moral code.
We do not mind our losses as
We steadily erode.

We do not mind the burning as
We lie upon the coals.
We do not mind the judgment as
We relegate our souls.

Apathy II

We do not mind "eternal" as
We live for what is now.
We do not mind the bleeding as
We see his thorn-crowned brow.
We do not mind his glory as
We turn to chase our own.
We do not mind author'ty as
We seek to claim the throne.
We do not mind his nature as
We throw away his law.
We do not mind perfection as
We magnify our flaw.
We do not mind his mercy as
We bask in our betray'l.
We do not mind foundation as
We fall back on the frail.
We do not mind sov'reignty as
We doubt his pow'r and will.
We do not mind the Giver as
We steal and rape and kill.

We do not mind the holy as
We make our master Sin.
We do not mind redemption as
We turn to death again.

An Invitation

The syllables I share with you are such
As cannot be conceived by mortal men.
These words of wisdom hold a holy touch;
When heeded, hell-bound souls are saved from sin
So that they are no longer bound for hell
But are, before the judge's throne, redeemed.
Those who are parched are pardoned at the well
By one who was not very much esteemed.
This revelation of the only way
Requires that we would a decision make.
The son that rose to shine the light of day
Has dawned that darkened souls might now awake.
Do not now spurn this love he came to give;
Choose you this day to turn to Christ and live.

Desensitized

Why do we find such follies fun
And magnify the madness?
The filth from which we ought to run
Fills us with giddy gladness.
So should we not expect to find
That love for God is lacking?
And in the church we are not kind
But are ourselves attacking?
Oh can we not reject the dross
And seek sanctification?
Do not, for "fun," reject the cross
Nor bask in your damnation.
For Christ has saved our souls from sin
That we might sin no longer.
Embrace his grace, his nail pierced skin,
And in his love grow stronger.

A Prayer of Pursuit

O Father, let me never be
A hindrance to your plan for me,
But grant me, Lord, the eyes to see
The roads you'd have me travel.
And strengthen me to follow thee
By sun or star, by land or sea,
Until the day I fin'lly flee
This world of grit and gravel.

Thought

I think we only think we think
When our imagination
Is captivated at the brink
Of some infatuation.
The meeting of the mind with wonder
Tricks us to assume
That old ideas are torn asunder,
New ideas to bloom.
But truly we have only just
Begun to chip away the rust
And wipe away the years of dust
For mental exploration.
And pushing past the stench of must,
Advancing with a forward thrust
Into the realms of doubt and trust,
We reach the elevation.
And it is there we find
A freedom for the mind

As God in grace unbinds
Our thoughts from Satan's blinds.
Press on! Press on! And think to know
The truth amidst the lies below!

Flesh and Spirit

I trust you, but I do not trust you;
Love you, but my heart is cold;
Hope in you, yet live as hopeless.
I am new, yet still am old.
I am your own by your good pleasure,
Living by your love and grace.
Why then do I dare to doubt and
In your presence hide my face?
O Father, how I still forsake you
While I wish to know you more.
Wretched flesh, this wayward servant,
Words to wrench me from your shore.
But it cannot defeat redemption,
Nor diminish your resolve.
None can snatch this great salvation,
Nor condemn those you absolve.
So in this grace I stand acquitted,
Salvaged from futility.
Now I live by thy great power
Free for all eternity.

Wisdom and Gain

Is it not gain to sacrifice
When giving to the Lord?
Since he has paid the ransom price,
Can we not love afford?
Is it not wise to lay aside
The things that pass away
And in the light of love abide
For this alone will stay?
Is it not loss to grasp and cling
For what can never fill,
And follow after hopes that bring
Destruction to the will?
Is it not foolishness to prize
What only will decay,
And feed the fault before our eyes
Which on our souls does prey?

The Treasures of Tragedy

O Father, I shudder with ev'ry affliction.
The day seems far dimmer than ever before.
Man is corrupted by sin's contradiction.
The depths of depravity darken my door.
I know of no road to escape this great testing.
The cries and the chaos do threaten demise.
Sickness and sorrow are my heart arresting,
But within this furnace is found a great prize.
The treasures of tragedy truly perplex me:
I sought not a one, yet I value them all.
Verily does this perplexity vex me,
But ne'er would I waste e'en a drop of this gall.
I wish to be rid of this cup so revolting.
God, with ev'ry draught, I am drinking in death.
Yet you have suffered a far worse assaulting,
And yet you are with me with every breath.
You sanctify me through the seasons of suff'ring.
When all else around me gives way, you remain.
God, 'gainst the enemy, you are my buff'ring,
And you will redeem ev'ry moment of pain.

Conviction

God, guide your Word like a sword for my reckoning,
Wrecking all hopes in my heart for this waste.
Cut to the quick for the purpose of quickening
Works of your Spirit to sever the sickening
Sludge that I sought in my haste.

Clauses like claws are accustomed to scratch away
Any remainder of wretchedness here.
Tear away sin and, in so doing, tear a way
Through the commotion that coaxes my heart astray
Till I have learned how to fear.

Let ev'ry phrase of your holy book break my heart
For ev'ry way I dishonor your name.
Never relent; pierce my soul from the very start
Till I reflect your resplendence with ev'ry part,
Living as proof of your claim.

Salvation

Oh come to the fountain, you fellows of folly,
Come to the well and be quenched of your thirst.
Our Lord has arranged through the firstborn's arrival
Rescue for souls who are captive and cursed.
Oh tarry no longer in Satan's dominion;
Reach out and touch as the hem passes by,
For faith in his power will prove to be pardon;
Hope in his healing he will not deny.
For all who are weary and burdened may meet him.
He condescended to show us the way.
Our vile captivation was crushed in his conquest.
He brought new life to these vessels of clay.

Evidence of Grace

I wonder whether *I am growing* here,
Or whether I am *day by day* the same.
I bow before his *Spirit showing* fear
While sin is showing *me the way* to shame.
Surrendering to *sanctifying* love,
I seek to know you *by your book* of truth.
Appearing as a *heart defying* dove,
You help my heart 'scape *ev'ry hook* of youth.
Yet still I wonder, *God of glory* bright,
How can I know that *you are here* to stay
When messages of *gospel music* fight
To work their way in *to my ear* of clay?
Might I gain access *to your kingdom* then?
To find the ev'dence, *I must look* within.

My Heart's Desire and Plea

I long for you to fin'lly see
The stains of this iniquity,
To recognize the travesty,
To turn to Christ, our hope and plea.
I pray for you to one day be
Reborn a child of royalty
So that you would be ever free
From sin's eternal poverty.
The curse's pow'r no more remains;
Christ's blood has cleansed the deepest stains.
He condescended to our pains;
Ascended, now forever reigns.
So you need not inhabit holes
Hewn by the hands of hostage souls.
Now turn your gaze to higher goals
As all creation now extols
The one who gave the beggar sight,
Forgave the wrong and showed the right,
Took up the sword and won the fight,
The incarnation of the light.

From. Through. To.

From him are all things:
Earth and sky and all thereof.
All creation clings
To the voice that called in love
Ev'ry sound that sings.

Through him are all things.
By his power he sustains
Ev'ry sound that sings.
Gifts of sunlight and of rains
Year by year he brings.

To him are all things:
His the glory and the throne.
All creation clings
To the king who hears the groan
And salvation brings.

The Subtle Subversion

Perceptions of obedience to Christ
Are often apprehended by our hopes,
And flesh, the lowly subject, turns to heist
And seeks to send true service to the ropes.
For in our work for glory, we presume
To warrant some promotion, pleasure, prize.
Desire conceived breeds sin within the womb.
The idol soon is fixed before our eyes.
Conviction then gives contest to the beast,
Reminding us that God is not so poor.
And we, in comfort, trust that he will give,
And see our Maker merely as a door.
Through subtlety the serpent can subvert
A heart for holiness to lust for dirt.

Contentions of Convictions

Truth is a subject often in dispute
When two interpretations disagree.
Two brothers – neither list'ning – turn to shoot
The other dead rather than bend the knee.
Assuming that there is no middle ground,
No chance that God is wiser than their minds,
They trip and trap and trigger all around
The body harsh divisions of all kinds.
And as the fights erupt, the mission fades
And is forgotten 'neath the cries of war.
The rescue ships no longer act as aids;
They leave the dying stranded on the short.
True doctrine does deserve our strong defense.
Contentions of convictions? Recompense.

A Prayer for Rescue

Cleanse me lest I perish, Lord.
Purify my lep'rous skin.
Break these hands that hurt and horde.
Save me from the curse of sin.
Tame this tongue that tears apart.
Wreck this will that seeks its own.
Now ignite my lifeless heart.
[Present death, be overthrown]
Turn your sword upon my soul.
Sever the deceiver's hold.
Have in me the full control.
Shatter visions of fool's gold
Till I learn to follow thee,
Walking in your righteous way.
Grant me, Lord, the eyes to see.
I surrender all today.

Purpose

Let my life be more than just existence.
Let me look beyond the day to day.
Teach me the importance of persistence
Till inner resistance falls away.
I am prone to wander, apt to tarry
When the time has come to carry on.
Be for me, therefore, a holy ferry
Through the night until the light of dawn.
Make me know the measure of my being.
Let me look beyond forgiven crimes.
With each passing moment, keep me seeing
Your eternity within our times.
May the purpose of this present moment
Far outweigh all former faults and fears.
Focus me in view of the atonement.
Fetter me to thee for all my years.

Faith's Effect

Success if measured not in thought alone,
Nor victory in mind's imagining.
Accomplishment is not emotion shown.
Fulfillment ne'er forsakes the offering.
But faith is evidenced by faithful deeds,
By empty pockets and by calloused hands.
Faith proves itself in prayer, in meeting needs,
In bringing light and love to darkened lands.
Faith stands against this present apathy
And challenges the heart of selfishness.
If Christ was crushed for sin instead of me,
Then let me never speak but to confess.
True faith compels me to apply the Word
And testify to Christ till all have heard.

Balance

O Father, help my heart to feel
The truth my mind affirms
And stop the doubts that seek to steal
The hope the truth confirms.
Secure in me the surety
Of your eternal hold
And pardon the impurity
Of my ill ways of old.
But neither let emotion rule –
It too is slavery –
For then I would be as the fool,
Storm-driven on the sea.
Grant me a balance by your Word
To walk the narrow way,
And let your guidance undergird
My life from day to day.

The Ghost

A boy who died when I was just a boy
Has haunted me up to this very day.
His ghost I fear I never will destroy;
His face I fear will never fade away.
With breathless voice, he whispers in my ear.
With sightless eyes, he stares into my soul.
With every step I take, I see him sneer
With devilish desire to take control.
But victory for him would mean my doom,
For he would see me suffering in hell.
Though safe am I by truth of empty tomb,
The specter whispers still, "All is not well."
I am until my final breath a host
Ever departing from him, my own ghost.

The Dark's Deception

There is a depth of darkness that, when found
Appears to the observer to be light,
A light so strange, so buried, yet so bright:
Illumination hidden in the ground.
The world to this observer all around
Appears as filtered through his altered sight,
Assures that he alone is in the right.
In time, his voice will be to him the sound
Of truth amidst the mass of ignorance.
His earth will seem to him a world of slaves
In need of him, the savior of mankind.
In truth, the darkness robbed him of his sense.
He cannot tell he walks among the graves
Of others who, like him, have been made blind.

The Culprit

The tempter set before the man a game.
"Three tries to name your greatest enemy.
If you succeed, this lion will be tame,
But if you fail, you never will be free."
The man thought for a moment then agreed.
"You are a devil, sir, and most unwise,
So I will take advantage and be freed."
From lips which grinned, the devil said, "Two tries."
Taken aback, the man said, "Satan, then."
And Satan, snickering, said, "Last attempt."
"Then Lucifer I name thee, lord of sin!"
Then you, sir, from sin's rule are not exempt."
This captive man will have to face God's thresh
Unless he will perceive his guilty flesh.

The Fear of the Lord

My eyes behold a sight so terrible
And lovely I cannot but stand in awe
And dread at knowing now what others saw,
The truth perceived in part through parable.
The Lord of all that is, in love and wrath,
Has ev'ry right to rid his world of me.
And I, now seeing him, do suddenly
Abandon all excuses for my path,
This road which led me to my own demise.
I am a sinful man deserving naught
But righteous condemnation without end.
Yet now I hear a spotless lamb's last cries,
And now I learn my worthless life is bought,
And now I know that Christ has called me friend.

A Prayer

Lead on, lead on, O sacred flame.
Bring light into the darkness.
Let me live wholly for your name
In movement as in stillness
That you might use my feeble frame
To show the world your greatness.

Temper

These fleeting frustrations can fill me with fury;
The littlest loss can produce a lament.
Please pardon this person so lost in the flurry;
Prevent me from spurning this chance to repent.

Let not limitations incite my impatience.
Impertinent thoughts – let them perish from me.
For I am a man unaffected by penance,
Provoked by the splinters I happen to see.

Yet you have forgiven my vilest offenses.
You made me a son though I spit in your face.
God, break down my barriers, dash my defenses,
And teach me to live by your mercy and grace.

Let me learn to better reflect your perfection.
Let sanctification reach every part.
Let my life bear witness to thy great salvation
As patience and peace rule my critical heart.

Grief

Broken with no hope of being mended.
Focused on a chapter that has ended.
Feeling as if time has been suspended.
Captivated by a sudden stillness.
Life appears infected with an illness.

Pain, oh how much longer will you tarry?
Fear: oppressive fog around the ferry.
How much farther, Father, must I carry
Weakness like a cancer in my being
Which corrupts the sights that I am seeing?

Deeply does the curse cause me to suffer.
With each passing day, the road feels rougher.
God, be my deliverance, my buffer.
I can not in my own strength endure this.
Must I suffer so much in your service?

Yet your promise holds, for you are working
All things for the good – even the hurting.
Keep me, then, in test and trial, from cursing
You in your unfathomable wisdom.
Keep me focused on your holy kingdom.

Lies

The master of deception posed a question:
"How best can I befuddle Adam's race?"
He chose to replicate God's holy bastion
With subtle changes only few would trace.
He calls the son of God a moral teacher
Whose lessons help us all live better lives.
The serpent thus can sabotage a preacher
And turn a church into a teeming hive
Of people bent on earning their salvation
By feeble works of their polluted hands.
Grace is avoided by the "able" nation
As death under the law engulfs all lands.
Or else the serpent says the Christ will save us
From any consequences from our sins.
Asserting this, the serpent can enslave us
To think that pain-free living now begins.
He whispers that if difficulty tarries,
We must not be believing well enough.
He, in this way, ensures the Christian carries
A heart of fear or a self-righteous bluff.
So listen well, my fellows, to the Scriptures

And flee the lying words which tempt the ear,
For catchy lines, which make for pretty pictures,
Are laced with hooks to kill, so learn to fear
All forms of "almost truth" and seek the certain.
Be on your guard no matter where you trod.
Trust in the Spirit, see beyond the curtain,
And walk in wisdom by the truth of God.

Wonder

You spoke, and all that is began to be,
Yet you are uncreated, without end.
The voice with which you rule eternity
Is present in the whisper of the wind.
In sov'reignty, you raise and lower kings.
No power can contest your ruling right,
For you are he of whom creation sings,
The power that ordains the day and night.
And yet you clothe the flowers of the ground,
And yet you feed the sparrows of the sky.
You care for your creation all around
So much you sent your sinless son to die.
It matters not how much I may rehearse:
Your greatness, God, I cannot grasp in verse.

Mortality

Life is but a vapor;
Time, a fading dream.
Length of days doth taper;
This, the common theme.
Ponder, then, your portance.
Perish not a breath.
Emphasize importance.
Think upon your death.
Contemplate eternal
Intersecting now.
See beyond external.
Vivify your vow.
Let the weight of glory
Grip your finite frame.
See the higher story.
Never be the same.

Life Till Death's Cessation

Stained with sin but for your grace, I
Long to look upon your face. Thy
Never-failing word commands my
Failing heart to focus. Faith is
Crying, "Father, stoke us. Take this
Weakened will in your hands." Of his
Life and death and life again, I
Sing, a breath midst strive and sin. Thy
Son resplendent understands my
War with this temptation. Such is
Life till death's cessation. In this
Hope my salvaged soul stands, all his.

Poetry

The gospel is the poetry of truth,
For in it love and beauty condescend
From heav'n above to take the form of youth:
A righteous life to cover those who sinned.
Redemption's plan was fixed before the fall.
The father, through his prophets, has foretold
The coming of the king who sounds the call
To all who under sin and death are sold.
Twas at the proper time and proper place
The son himself engaged man's greatest foe,
And, by his death, the dead were made alive.
Alive again, the word of love and grace
Inaugurates his kingdom here below,
And all who know him evermore shall thrive.

Grieving Well

Pain is not without its purpose.
Tragedy still points to truth.
Terror may seem to usurp us,
Yet our God is not uncouth.
He, in sovreignty, is moving.
Evil cannot halt his will.
Through the darkness, he is proving
Faithful. Let us then be still.
Nothing from his gaze is hidden.
He will never fail or tire.
Evils come to us unbidden;
Evil will one day expire.
Suffer well, O worn believer.
See the larger plan unfold.
Trust the Father, blessed receiver.
He is purging you like gold.

Fear and Faith

My final destination is secured;
Tis fixed within my future by the pow'r
Sustaining all creation ev'ry hour.
And yet the days ahead appear obscured.
By pages and by principles applied,
May I perchance perceive the Father's plan
(And thus pursue the path by strength of man
And live a life untested and untried)?
No. Faith is forged by following in fear,
Uncertain of the details of the road
Yet certain of the Master's love and might.
Help me then, Lord, to listen and to hear.
Let me abide in thee in this abode
And learn to walk by faith and not by sight.

Words for the Wind

I take up pen and page to point to truth
And pray my purpose is not rendered vague.
I recognize my mind reveals my youth;
Lord, let me neither tarry nor stravage.
I am a humble runnel of your reign.
Use these, my words, like water to refresh.
And when I feel my writing is in vain,
Remind me that I do not write for flesh.
These poems need not please the multitude.
These words require no mortal praise nor fame.
These messages may never earn my food;
I pray they ever glorify your name.
I write to please the one who knows my end.
I offer these, my poems for the wind.

Transition

Another chapter closes now, and I
Lay down my pen to catch a bit of breath.
I reminisce o'er days that have gone by
And look ahead to days until my death.

Through weeks and months and years, you did unfold
The plan that brought me to this present time,
And though you took things I had hoped to hold,
Your rule has brought about a better rhyme.

I trust you with the days that are ahead;
I still will follow though I cannot see.
Perfection bore the wages in my stead;
I do not doubt your daily love for me.

This marker on the road lifts up my face,
A testimony to your truth and grace.

Reflection

I see my lack of holiness
When I observe my heart.
It shows a certain homelienss:
Tis stained in ev'ry part.
I long to live in purity
Yet clearly not enough,
For sin remains a surety.
Temptation calls my bluff.
Thus I take up these robes of white;
I drag them through the dirt.
I pledged my life to perfect light,
Yet still pursue my hurt.
Oh pardon me this parody,
This purposeless pursuit.
Enable me to fully be
A son who bears good fruit.
May all who hear my story find
Your mark of perfect love,
And use me, Father, to remind
Them of your land above.

Job

See him, possessing all good things,
Continuing his offerings.
Take careful note of how he sings.
His is a heart that knows its place.
He recognizes all is grace
And loves his unseen Father's face.

See him now, hearing all are lost.
Into a storm his soul is tossed.
The friends who comfort soon accost.
Now pay attention to the cast,
For though prosperity has past,
His resignation still holds fast.

See him, bereft of all good things,
Still praising through his sufferings.
Take careful note of how he sings.
His is a heart that knows its place.
He recognizes all is grace
And loves his unseen Father's face.

Anthropomorphize

We call our urges animal,
And thus we may explain them all away.
What once was seen as black and white
Is now seen certainly as simply grey.
Could such desires be criminal
If we too far beyond the limits stray?
Or might it be that wrong and right
Run deeper than what our emotions say?

Misdirected Worship

We are a people prone to adulation
Who often are audacious with our praise.
Provoking conflagration, we
Resist all abrogation. See!
The idols are the masters of our days.
Such worship is a devastating blaze.

Idolatry is no anachronism.
All ages suffer its asperity.
Discern the serpent's schism.
See the apposite baptism. We
Reject apocryphal authority
And trade acerbic lies for clarity.

Presence

The presence of my shepherd is my peace.
His goodness to me day by day, my song.
His love for me bids all my worries cease.
He over ev'ry enemy is strong.
I lack no needed thing, for he is here
In deepest darkness as in brightest light.
Amid my enemies, I do not fear,
For God, my father, watches through the night.
No storm or sword or snake can separate
My soul from the Almighty's sov'reign grasp.
This body may decay, these doubts berate –
Still I remain within my father's clasp.
True life is life lived at the shepherd's side.
I make it thus my aim to there abide.

A Prayer for Wisdom and Humility

I do not know how much I do not know.
I know that there are limits to my reach.
Let me, O Lord, as I aspire to teach,
Walk in humility and ever grow.
Let fear protect me from presumption's throes
And keep me bowed before your holy face.
Teach me to dwell before your throne of grace.
Speak heaven's poetry to human prose.
My learning threatens me with arrogance.
It whispers lies of self-sufficiency
And hides the truth I know, that I am weak.
Grant me a reverential reticence.
Produce in me humble proficiency.
God, make me quick to hear and slow to speak.

Prone to Wander

I knew you once to be a flame
Bright with heaven's joys,
But now it seems twas all a game.
You mock the faith you once did claim,
Chasing after toys
(Ephemeral treasures) and fame.

Reflections on Psalm 39

Oh know your place, my soul.
Remember that your days are view.
Tis vanity
To live with just this age in view.
Relinquish your control.

Eternal God most high,
Provide perspective to my days.
Tis vanity
To live in conflict to your ways
As death draws ever nigh.

Reflections on Psalm 50

At the word of the Maker, the earth
Is brought forth to revolve round the sun
To the praise and the glory of one
Who possesses an infinite worth.
He shines forth from perfection's high'st form,
From great Zion with sounds of a choir.
Ev'ry step is preceded by fire;
When he walks, he is shrouded in storm.
His salvation is given, not bought,
For he owns all that we could present.
Sacrifices for vices are spent,
Yet they profit the Almighty naught.
So walk not in the pathways of death.
Ponder life 'fore your lips claim his pow'r.
Let the fear of the Lord fill each hour,
And let thanksgiving fill ev'ry breath.

Transformation

Proper fear begets a proper faith.
The foreigner becomes family.
God gives substance to the wraith:
Glorious anomaly.
Grace and mercy meet the guilty heart
Turning stone to living flesh and blood.
Love transforms every part,
Cleansing in the crimson flood.

The Lamb, The Lion

The sacrificial lamb was laid upon
The altar by the hands of wicked men,
And all was dark the days before the dawn
In the apparent victory of sin.
The lesser lion, seeking to devour,
Set his assault against the sacred son,
And Satan, in the darkness of the hour,
Was certain that the victory was won.
And so it was, but not for his array.
The cross of Christ displayed for all to see
That Satan's claim to power had been wrong.
The finished hunter had become the prey.
The word made flesh fulfilled the prophecy.
The lamb had been a lion all along.

Redemption's Rhyme

Within this world of fiction,
I yearn for heaven's diction
To deepen my conviction.

I feel the present friction
From our great self-infliction,
And long for sin's eviction.

Though strong the serpent's striction,
He faces grave restriction
In all of his affliction.

For Christ, the great nonfiction,
God's visible depiction,
Fulfilled the Word's prediction.

The Practice of Prayer

O Father, how I struggle so
To come before your throne.
In public, pray'r oft turns to show;
In private, how I drone.
Though you twice o'er gave life to me,
I come still wanting more –
Unwarranted expectancy
Now knocking at your door.
No more.
Let thine own will alone be done,
And let thy kingdom come.
Let me in life reflect the Son,
To love and be not numb.
Grant that my tastes are tempted not
By poverty nor wealth.
Peace and forgiveness, be my lot;
Humility, my health.
O Father who in heaven dwells
In holiness and light,
Keep me away from worthless wells,
From trusting in my might.

God, grant me eyes to recognize
Your grandeur and your grace.
Teach me to treasure you as prize,
And ever seek your face.

The Problem of Evil

As history has been unfurled,
One question 'gainst the church has stood:
From whence came evil to this world
If God created all things good?
We grant some evil works for gain,
Some purpose may be found therein;
Yet is there not much needless pain,
Much suffering because of sin?
Could God not keep his world from death,
Or (bitter thought), might he desire
To curse those he hath filled with breath,
To see them sinking in the mire?
Or might it be that he allows
His people to rebel, to stray,
That they may truly then avow
His lordship, then may truly pray?
And could it be that majesty
Did not abandon to decay
Damned souls, but there upon the tree
Engaged in full the sinner's fray?
Christ bore the wrath of God in place

Of those who chose the path to hell
That they might turn to seek the face
Of love, to taste the one true well.
God's justice cometh like a flame,
And evil will not stand the show.
I may not know from whence it came,
But I know well where it will go.

Perspective

The heart that hurts to hold the hand
Of one who shares both heart and name
Can only ever understand
The purpose past the painful game
By fixing eyes upon the Lord
Who sov'reignly provides for needs
And knowing that the piercing sword
Is severing the sickly weeds
Which would corrupt the growing fruit
For which we labor, trust, and pray.
God sees the garden at the root
And guides us toward the light of day.

Atonement

Christ upon the tree.
Christ in place of me.
Bearing heaven's righteous wrath.
Sacred Son's blood: cleansing bath.
Salvaging my heart for thee
Clarified the path.

Reminder

Soul, be silent. Listen well.
Hope in God and pray.
He who saved your soul from hell
Will bring you through this day.
Worry never. Doubt him less.
Know that he is God.
Learn to live in humbleness
And trust your shepherd's rod.
Fix your focus. Do not shirk.
Stand as he has stood.
He will cause all things to work
Together for your good.
If this day should end in death,
Sing the last refrain.
Faithful to the final breath,
At last, to die is gain.

Alone

I am alone,
No one beside me 'fore the throne.
All come and go,
And so I turn my heart to stone
And stay alone.

I am alone.
Emotion seems a worthy price.
Just let it go,
Embrace the noble sacrifice.
Remain alone.

And yet, I feel.
I am alone, and incomplete.
And as I go,
I long to hear some other feet.
I want to feel.

I do not see
How these desires can e'er be met,
But I will go
And pray for faith to never fret
Till I can see.

Fear and Faith

I strive to walk not by my sight
But by my faith, for such is right;
But sight so terrifies my soul
For I am never in control.
My will is weak, my focus frail;
My future hope, in them, is pale.
My understanding fails to find
A footing, for my eyes are blind.

When all around me calls for fear,
To gospel truth I turn my ear.

God still is on his throne above,
Still steadfast in his perfect love.
His pow'r to rule, affected naught
By my imperfect, doubting thought.
No fear of failure, want of strength,
Nor any trial of any length

Can sever heaven's holy grip
Upon my soul, this sinking ship.
I know, though I know not the path,
That God, in sov'reign mercy, hath
Made straight the road and called me to
His purpose, which is ever true.

Dextrocardia

We may not sense the abnormality,
For our appearance does not show the flaw;
But let us look within and we will see
A core not in accord with natural law.
Our symptoms show themselves in varied ways,
Outward effects which hint at inner fault.
All people, fixed and fallen, offer praise,
But differ in the objects they exalt.
And thus most men believe that they are whole,
For they, with eyes untrained, cannot detect
The devastating sickness in the soul
Which works to their eternity infect.
Our only hope is heaven's holy art,
The surgeon who can fix a backwards heart.

Unfailing Faithfulness

The Lord's unfailing faithfulness to men,
Steadfast in spite of their consistent sin,
Goes far beyond the guilt and shame within.
Grace reaches past the point of no return.
Hope speaks from lips we thought were taciturn.
We hear the Word, and souls begin to burn.
We know what we deserve; we feel our death.
We sense our separation from his life.
Yet though we fail with ev'ry fallen breath,
In Christ, we find salvation from the strife.
Take heart: this world of fear and death will fade.
Rest in the cross's sanctifying shade.

Wait

For what do I wait when I wait?
Do I lack the strength to complete
The journey before me? Does fate
Require more merit? Oh, this heat
Makes me restless. How long must I
Stay, unmoving as the process
Purifies me of worldly dye?
How long, O Lord? For I confess
I long to run. This surgery
May mend, but how it hurts me so!
I wonder, would you murder me
To purge the sin which lives below?
(Perhaps tis so.)
When can I go? When will this end,
This sanctification, this flame?
You who eternally transcend
My thoughts and ways, your holy name
Is both my hope and bane. I break
Before your unrelenting hand
Which works to my foundations shake
Until I trust in your command.

So have your way in me, I pray.
Though I may never comprehend
Your purpose, let me near you stay,
O God, the absolute, my end.

The Word and The Heart

Your word: my great undoing, my delight.
I fear to look within, yet fear to stray,
For fear of you (sweet wisdom) shines a light
Upon my path and forces me to say
That I know not my heart or mind so well
As I assumed. This flesh doth e'er deceive.
No strength of will nor want could ever quell
Its tenor regnant. I cannot relieve
My soul from waywardness, for I am bound.
In ev'ry song I sing, I hear its sound.
Discern, speak truth, correct! Let me be found!
You see more clearly than I ever could
And cut more deeply than I wish you would.
I know that all of this is for my good.

Process

Though the night be filled with bitter sorrow,
Joy comes in the mourning, in the waiting,
In the ignorance, the hesitating.
In our times of testing, God is calling
Those with ears to hear to heed his whisper.
We perceive our need when we start falling
Then detect the Spirit's voice grow crisper.
God, in perfect love, exposes fiction.
House of cards collapsed then on the table.
He reveals to us with clearest diction
That we need him and that he is able
To, in our great weakness, show his power,
Quenching not the wick nor crushing flower.
Hope then, soul, for God controls tomorrow.

Incarnation

Preeminent yet immanent, the Christ,
The holy word, the light, the lion-lamb,
Emptied himself to soon be sacrificed
In order to redeem and not to damn
The sin-stained souls of all who would believe
In heaven's gift of peace and righteousness.
The angels sing! Rejoice, all you who grieve!
The Lord has come this day to save, to bless!
Behold the babe born to our soil and sod,
The timeless son translated into time,
The image of the invisible God,
The all transcendent Lord's audible rhyme.
The infant in the manger you now see?
Upholder of the universe is he.

Humility and Grace

Might sins which seem so far removed from us
Be those which pose the greatest hidden threat?
Temptations that we never much discuss
May be o'erlooked, which leads us to forget
To strengthen our defenses 'gainst the foes.
Imagining that we, somehow exempt
From diff'rent dangers, will not face such woes,
We look on those who struggle with contempt.
In truth, we are no better off than they,
For we all wrestle with the fallen state.
We all would perish if not for the Way.
We all need God to make our pathways straight.
So guard your heart with all humility,
Or else risk falling to futility.

Humility

My eyes, too weak to properly perceive
The face of beauty, found in God alone,
See clearly lesser things, and thus they leave
The truth of God for gods of self and stone.
And thus I grow to hold too high a place
In my own estimation. I forget
That any good in me is all of grace.
My ev'ry breath is evidence of debt
To God who is the giver of the breath,
Revealed in part, unknowable in whole.
He is, before my birth, beyond my death,
The maker and sustainer of my soul.

Adjust my eyes to greater glories see;
Thereby produce in me humility.

A Prayer for Faith

Focus me in faith to follow
You no matter where you lead me.
Let my doctrine be not hollow.
Keep me ever near thee.

Sov'reignty will not be over-
Turned. I need not ever worry.
God, who clothes the fleeting clover,
Never needs to hurry.

The Paradox of Flesh

The flesh is weak, and thus the flesh is strong.
Its eyes, created to behold the light,
Look to be filled by shadows in the night.
Its lips attempt to sing a lesser song,
Changing its subject to subjects. Its hands
Fight to feel control. Its nose calls rotten
All fragrance of the only begotten.
Its mind feigns thought yet never understands.
Strange is its weakness, stranger still its strength,
For, though inferior to its design,
The flesh oft captivates the soul of man,
Distracting all the senses for the length
Of life, lest spirit somehow glimpse a sign
That life was purposed for a higher plan.
Ne'er underestimate the danger here.
Long as you live, the enemy is near.

Comparison

Compare at your own peril, for your life
Will never measure up to what you see
In others. You will only grow in strife.
You build a prison cell though you are free.
When we compare, we only see in part.
We view another's gain where we have naught.
We note the diff'rences but miss the art
Of walking in the Way the master taught.
O faulty vision, warped by my desire,
Look not to other men but to the Lord.
Comparison would be to me a fire,
And its destruction I cannot afford.
So fight, my soul, temptations to compare
Or else resign to living in despair.

Death and Life

Death will come for all men in the end.
None escape the final reckoning.
All who climb the mountains must descend.
All must heed th'eternal beckoning.
Righteous men and wicked men alike
Fade at last into obscurity.
Actions matter not, for doom will strike
All the grave remains a surety.

Is there gain in doing what is good?
Can we earn a single day of bliss?
We still die in doing what we should.
Vanity of vanities is this.

Yet the story need not end in vain.
Death does not possess the highest pow'r.
Life embodied died to end death's reign.
Now we need not fear the final hour.
Slain upon a skull and then entombed,
Life partook in full the fatal drink.
Life then rose again, the curse consumed.

Hope now lives and nevermore will sink.
Therefore we have purpose in our ways,
For we follow him who doth transcend.
Christ has given meaning to our days.
Now we know that death is not the end.

Holy Alteration

You save us from idolatry
Through disappointment.
The call to bear the killing tree
Is healing ointment.
"Take up your cross and follow me" –
Divine appointment.

We do not know the depths of sin
Within our being.
We fight against but cannot win;
But you, all seeing,
Stepped into time to work for men
Eternal freeing

From forces that devise the fall
Of your creation.
Depravity common to all
Met its damnation.
Now hear, all broken hearts, his call:
Propitiation.

In you, we hope. For you, we wait.
You, the provider.
You know our weakness, our estate;
Your grace is wider.
You bear our sin and fix our fate,
Divine divider.

Fruit

Love displayed in life laid down for others.
Joy surpassing all this earth can offer.
Peace before both enemies and brothers.
Patience with the doubter and the scoffer.
Kindness to all creatures in creation.
Goodness shining brightly through corruption.
Faithfulness becomes our firm foundation.
Gentleness endures despite disruption.
Self-control o'er all the flesh's passion.
Self-deni'l, a daily crucifixion.
Faith e'er growing more in holy fashion.
Truth proclaimed with notes of heaven's diction.
Spirit, lead our walking, guide our living.
Let the world see you in our thanksgiving.

A Witness

Do flowers honor Father more than I?
For they do not rebel against his name,
Never abandon purpose to proclaim
Another glory. Ev'ry passerby
Is bidden by the bud to look beyond,
To glimpse the author of the grand design.
I point as well, but I demand a fine,
Some profit for the prophet. Still, the frond
Is ever faithful. Though its days are few,
Great kings cannot compare to its array,
A testimony from the soil and sod.
Look closely and detect the divine hue
And find the same at work within your clay.
All beauty bears the signature of God.

Arguments

Lord, save me from the fatal flaw
Of needing to be right,
Of loving not my brother but the fight.
God, humble me with holy awe.
Let truth be my delight.
Let me persuade with meekness, not with might.

The Music

The dissonance resounds
As all attempt to sing
A song of their own making.
Disorder now abounds
For all forget the king
(A fatal undertaking).
We sing our dirge till death
Yet sing with all our might,
Our very voices breaking.
With ev'ry selfish breath,
We shrink away from light
To try to stop the aching.
But light shines in the dark,
And dark cannot resist.
The kingdom is advancing.
There is a holy ark.
With joy, we may subsist.
Salvation comes with dancing.
Amidst the rebel choir,
A melody is heard
That rings throughout creation.

The true composer's ire
Fell full upon the word:
Perfect propitiation.
The ransomed sing his song
Now knowing it involves
The rescue of the dying.
Though so much now seems wrong,
The song at last resolves:
Unending glorifying.

Easter

Father, let me ne'er forget the story
Of the cross, the tomb, the third day's glory.
For after those four hundred years so long,
Elijah's call was heard throughout the land.
"The kingdom comes! Repent! Make straight the way!"
And with his words, John pointed to the Word,
The spotless lamb of God, the virgin's son,
The heir to David's throne, the promised one.
He brought us peace yet also brought a sword;
The people were divided in that day.
They cried. He died. They did not understand.
He rose, and this is evermore our song:
The king has won the war we could not fight;
The darkness has not overcome the light.

Prayer for Humility

Let them know me not for my mind
Or my manners. Keep from them all
Tendency to love my name (kind
Flattery). Their praise is my fall,
For I know my heart enough to
Predict its vain response. They call
For me, and I shamefully do
All that I can to earn their awe.
I must decrease. I must decrease,
For I, though only briefly, saw
Your glory. Arrogance must cease,
For you alone warrant all fear
And worship. You who dwell above
Creation yet art ever near,
You meet us with your perfect love.
I am undone. Let me, then, be
A humble vessel. Let my boast
Be only of your grace to me.
O Father, Son, and Holy Ghost,
This clay can claim no title.

You Alone are worthy. Let all eyes
That look on me always see through
And your great glory recognize.
Be evident in all I do.

Christ

The fall was not the final word.
Isaiah has foretold,
A silent lamb shall take our place,
A saving act of wrath and grace
That sinners young and old
Might know the power of the Word.
Christ.
He laid aside his majesty
To be for us the light
And tasted death in place of men
That man might know freedom from sin.
He overcame the night
And shines for all eternity.

Fulfillment

Elusive fulfillment, promising much,
Master of anticipation and lust,
Warping a want till it feels like a must,
How many more must be crushed in your clutch?
Questioning you grows progressively more
Treacherous, for you twist my desiring
From pure motives in holy retiring
To meaner modes. I cease to see the war.

Awaken me, O Spirit. Help me hear
The still, small voice reminding me the way
To fullness is to seek a higher end.
My God, you reign. Teach me to love and fear,
To trust in your provision for this day,
And to abide in thee, most faithful friend.

Seeds

He knows our needs.
He promised to provide.
So worry not,
Nor let your courage fail.
Flow'rs grow from seeds
After the seeds have died.
You will not rot.
In Christ you will prevail.

Glory

Unmatched, unmarred by sin, unshaken, God
Maintains the utmost glory. 'Fore his face
E'en angels hide their faces. In that place
Corruption is not suffered, cannot trod
The ground made holy by his presence. Hide
Your eyes; gain clarity. Be still and know
That he is LORD o'er all, above, below.
Fear fills us, fear fulfills us: terrified
In tenderness. Unknown yet known; most high;
E'er near; eternally enthroned above
All enemies, all not-gods, perfect love
Perfectly conquers all, never runs dry.
The sun is but a shadow of his light.
No darkness can present a worthy fight.

Freedom

Why? Why, dear souls, do we insist
On clinging to our chains?
We who now wear robes which persist,
Why love we still the stains?
Christ bore the wrath our sin had earned.
No fear of death remains.
Forsake the things in Christ you spurned,
These passions and these pains.
For freedom, Christ has set us free,
And we are free indeed
From ev'ry subtle slavery
And ev'ry stifling weed.
No longer do we bear the curse
Of final poverty.
Heed now the joyful second verse:
Holy eternity.

Three Days

Remember now the darkness of those three long days
    before
The dawning of the day of resurrection,
For few have felt the fear of thinking God had lost the
    war.
The shadow of his people's insurrection
Now loomed across the future. Now our hope seemed
    spent and slain.
The light of life appeared to be extinguished.
The ones who sang his praises now in shock sang no
    refrain.
His life, howe'er, was willingly relinquished.
What seemed to be a sure defeat was fixed before the fall.
The devil's darkest scheme was his undoing.
As Christ was lifted up, he drew all men to heed his call.
He drained the cup of wrath our sin was brewing.
The bitter silence of that Sabbath day must have been
    great.
Unheard, Satan's presumpt'ous celebration.
When was it Satan realized the cross had sealed his fate?
The slaughtered lamb became our faith's foundation.

We now look back in wonder at this work in history
And sing with joy to God who reigns eternal.
The cornerstone came forth again in holy victory
O'er ev'ry sin, the mean and the infernal.
The resurrection of the Son secured our joy and peace.
No enemy can sabotage or sever
Us from the Father's love. In him, sin's slavery must
  cease.
Sing praise, his people, now and to forever.

Idols

Little children, keep yourselves from idols,
Works of our own hands. Voices – our voices –
Call us to cast off all righteous bridles,
Chastise us for limiting our choices.
Choose you then this day your lord, your master.
Choose the voice you trust above all others.
Choose the path to life, avoid disaster.
Heed the voice of reason, sisters, brothers.
Learn distrust of self, for self is often
Led astray by varied vices. Passions
Harden hearts to truth. Consciences soften,
Filled with fleshly fears and fleeting fashions.
Build upon the only sure foundation.
Idols only lead you to starvation.

Patience

Patience is a discipline I need, for I am sickly.

Patience is a virtue that I do not wish to learn.

Patience in this time of testing cannot come too quickly.

Patience, keep me when the passions burn.

Lament for the Forgotten Word

Stationary stationery
Lettered by blood. Word conceived; breathed;
Unread; unknown (momentary
Matters appear more pressing). Sheathed
Stays the saving sword, soul's defense
Lowered, life left unguarded. Lost
Direction. Subscribed to false sense
Of security, of the cost
Of trading truth and life and way
For pirate's treasure: cursed, unclean,
Corrosive to these hearts of clay
So fragile. Unperceived, unseen,
Light under a basket, hidden
City on a hill: no help, no
Sanctity, no sin forbidden.
Soon food for the father below.

The Crucible

The hearts of men may not detect
Distinctions 'twixt a noble trait
And meaner ones. They thus effect
No proper fight against the state
Of their impurity. But God
Knows well what yet resides within
The cage of bone and flesh. His rod
Gives direction and discipline
To wayward men that they may be
Saved from the state of sinfulness.
Corruption, at his word, must flee –
Proximity of holiness.
So fear not God's refining fire.
Let go the inexcusable.
Follow the path out from the mire
And trust the holy crucible.

They March

Harsh battle cries and cries from battle blows
Break full upon the ears by helmets hidden.
The enemy's assaults – always unbidden –
Besiege the soldiers. All around them, foes
Fling flaming arrows 'gainst the humble few.
The few still march, past bodies spoiled and sodden,
In search of captive souls. These, the downtrodden,
Still march, unbroken, victory in view.
They taste their own blood, wear blood not their own,
Press forward by a blood more diff'rent still.
They war to see the day the war will cease.
Though sore-afflicted, fire burns in their bone
To march with life no enemy can kill,
Their ev'ry step in war, a step t'ward peace.

Hebrews 11

If faith is an assurance, a conviction,
Then what is faith: an object or an action?
And what makes faith, according to depiction,
The only hope for holy satisfaction?

In days of old, our fathers knew your glory
And, knowing you, knew better their own measure.
Believing you would write the better story,
They walked by faith, and they received your pleasure.

Perhaps, then, faith is more than merely hoping;
'Tis certainty of forthcoming salvation.
E'en in our darkest days, we are not groping
But standing, grounded in a sure foundation.

Faith knows its Master, loves and fears his being.
This God invisible, faith's eyes are seeing.

Why Do I Write?

Why do I write?
I write to clarify my thoughts,
To contemplate the mights and oughts
For better sight.
Why do I write?
My voice and tongue do oft impede
Communication. Come and read
My soul's expression, for I need
To be transparent. I must heed
The call and write.
Why do I write?
I feel unable to convey
Emotion any other way.
These fears and joys that fill the day
I write at night.
Why do I write?
I draw near to the throne of grace
With pen and paper 'fore my face
To speak to you in humbler pace,
Requesting help to run the race,
To walk in light.

Why do I write?
I write to share what I have found
That some, by reading, might abound.
Therefore, I write.

ACKNOWLEDGMENTS

I want to thank my English professors for helping me to develop a love of words and of poetry in particular. Thank you to Dustin, Will, Jeff, Kevin, and Cade for their continual support as well as for their poem challenge suggestions. And thank you to Joe Fontenot for suggesting I compile some poems into a book and then for helping me to make this book possible. I thank the Lord for you all.

Five Round Rocks Media exists
as a resource for the church. Learn more at
FiveRoundRocksMedia.com.

Made in the USA
Coppell, TX
23 January 2021